The Planet Of The Grapes

Show Biz Jokes and Riddles

Compiled by Charles Keller
Illustrated by Mischa Richter

PIPPIN PRESS
New York

For Nicole and Leigh

Published by Pippin Press, 229 East 85th Street,
Gracie Station Box #92, New York, N.Y. 10028

Printed in the United States of America
by Horowitz/Rae Book Manufacturers, Inc.

10 9 8 7 6 5 4 3 2 1

Library of Congress Cataloging-in-Publication Data

Keller, Charles.
    The planet of the grapes : show biz jokes and
riddles / compiled by Charles Keller : illustrated by
Mischa Richter.
    Summary: Humor relating to the movie world,
sports, television, and other areas of the
performing arts.
    ISBN 0-945912-17-X :
    1. Riddles, Juvenile.   2. Performing arts—
Juvenile humor.   [1. Performing arts—Wit and
humor.   2. Jokes.   3. Riddles.]   I. Richter,
Mischa, ill.
PN6371.K44   1992
818'.5402—dc20   91-46550
                                                              CIP
                                                               AC

What's round, purple and orbits the sun?
The Planet of the Grapes.

What's the coolest row at the theater?
The Z-row.

What do you call a skinny detective?
Sherlock Bones.

If a king sits on gold, who sits on silver?
The Lone Ranger.

What formal suit does Donald Duck wear?
A duck-sedo.

Which two vegetables fight crime?
Beetman and Radish.

How does a television detective sneeze?
"A-clue! A-clue!"

What did Cinderella say to the photographer?
"Someday my prints will come."

What do you call a monster stomping through a swamp?
Bog Foot.

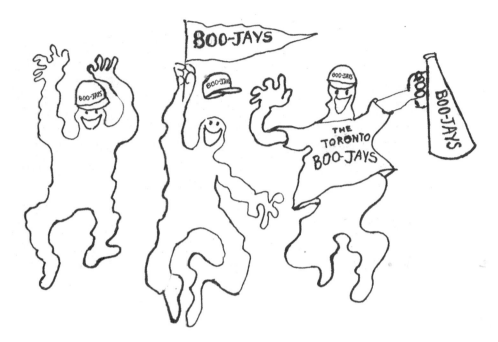

What baseball team do ghosts like best?
The Toronto Boo-Jays.

What keeps Star Trek going?
Spock plugs.

What did Yoda say to Snow White?
"May the dwarfs be with you."

What's a bug's favorite TV show?
"Fly Witness News."

What's the easiest way to get on television?
Sit on your set.

How did Edison's invention affect us?
If it weren't for him, we'd all be watching
television by candlelight.

Why did the man die at the drive-in?
He went to see "Closed for the Season."

What detective takes bubble baths?
Sherlock Foams.

What's round, flat, can fly, and has maple syrup on it?
Peter Pancake.

Why was the invisible man depressed?
He was all dressed up and had no face to go.

What do you call a monster baseball game?
The All-Scare Game.

What's the hardest thing to sell to a zombie?
Life insurance.

Who was Snow White's brother?
Egg White. Get the yoke?

Where do cows go for entertainment?
To the moo-vies.

What's a hamburger's favorite movie director?
Sizzle B. DeMille.

What would you do if an elephant sat in front of you at the movies?
Miss most of the picture.

How many letters are in the alphabet?
Twenty-four. E.T. went home.

Why does Batman wear pajamas?
He doesn't have a bat-robe.

What kind of glasses does James Bond wear?
Spy focals.

What happened when the invisible man married the invisible woman?
The children were nothing to look at.

Why does a Ninja Turtle never forget?
Turtle recall.

What honks and sings "Born in the U.S.A."?
Goose Springsteen.

What did one Hollywood fly say to the other?
"I just passed my screen test."

What's green, bumpy, and faster than a speeding bullet?
Super Pickle.

Why did the Wicked Witch ride a broomstick to her castle?
The extension cord on her vacuum cleaner wasn't long enough.

Why was Cinderella thrown off the baseball team?
She ran away with the ball.

What do you find at the end of Moby Dick?
A whale of a tail.

What kind of shoes does Mickey Mouse wear?
Squeakers.

What do you get when you cross a gorilla with a hammer?
King Kong.

What did Frankenstein say when he ran out of electricity?
"A.C. come, A.C. go."

How do gophers entertain themselves?
They watch underground movies.

Why did Godzilla eat Tokyo instead of Mexico City?
Because Mexican food gives him indigestion.

What did the director say after shooting the mummy movie?
"Wrap it up."

What's the most dangerous job in Transylvania?
Being Count Dracula's dentist.

What did the comedian say when he took off his clothes?
"Haven't you ever seen a comic strip?"

What keeps out bugs and shows movies?
Screens.

What did Batman have for lunch?
Alpha-bat soup.

What's the quietest sport on television?
Bowling—you can hear a pin drop.

What do monster children call their parents?
Mummy and Deady.

What was Samuel Clemens's pen name?
He never had a name for his pen.

Why does Dr. Jekyll go south for the winter?
To tan his Hyde.

What kind of TV program is shown early in the morning?
A breakfast serial.

Who was the boy puppet who whirled like a top?
Spinocchio.

Who did the Little Mermaid date?
She went out with the tide.

How did they find out how the Long Ranger voted in the election?
He left a silver ballot.

Why do television companies' teams win football games?
Because they have so many receivers.

Who has antlers and eats cheese?
Mickey Moose.

What's the first thing Dracula went to see when he visited New York?
The Vampire State Building.

What do you get when you cross a teddy bear with a skunk?
Winnie the Phew.

How do cowboy movie stars ride around?
In a cattle-act.

What happened when the prisoners put on a show?
It was a cell-out.

What's a robot's favorite snack in a science fiction movie?
Computer chips.

What do you call a race track in outer space?
A star track.

Why was Cinderella such a bad basketball player?
She had a pumpkin for a coach.

What's Jaws' favorite food?
A submarine sandwich.

Who did the movie popcorn salute?
The kernel.

How did the puppet get into show business?
His friend pulled a few strings for him.

What's a moose's favorite TV show?
"Mooster Rogers's Neighborhood."

What's Mickey Mouse's favorite breakfast?
Mice Krispies.

What do you call an airplane that flies backward?
An error plane.

What would ring if Arnold Schwarzenegger was at your front door?
The bar-bell.

What's a robot's favorite kind of music?
Heavy metal.

What's a pig's favorite television game show?
"Squeal of Fortune."

Who solved the murder of the Jolly Green Giant?
Celery Queen.

Why did Mickey Mouse take a trip to outer space?
To find Pluto.

What's a cat's favorite play?
"Ro-meow and Juliet."

How do you make a milk shake?
Take it to a scary movie.

Why did Mary get a job selling popcorn at the movies?
So she could be Mary Poppin.

How do you fasten a Ninja Turtle to a skateboard?
With a terra-pin.

What do grizzly detectives look for?
The bear facts.

Will Christmas trees grow in Los Angeles?
No, but Hollywood.

What does Garfield the Cat put on his hot chocolate?
Mousemellows.

What does Bugs Bunny get when he goes to the barber shop?
A hare-cut.

Where do spies do their shopping?
At a snooper market.

What kind of girl does the mummy go out with?
Any girl he can dig up.

How did the robbers in "Home Alone" break into the house?
Intruder window.

Why didn't Lassie run two miles to pick up a stick?
He thought it was farfetched.

Why did the cowboy aim his gun at the fan?
He was just shooting the breeze.

Which television channel has the best horror shows?
The Ghost to Ghost network.

What does Homer Simpson eat for lunch at the power plant?
Fission chips.

How did the Wicked Witch break the sound barrier?
With a sonic broom.

Why did Mrs. Claus bring her umbrella to the movies?
Because it may rain-deer.

How does Barbie like her hot dogs?
Barbie-cued.

What kind of television program tells you who just broke a leg?
A newscast.

Where does the Little Mermaid sleep?
In her water bed.

What do you call a pretty girl using a broom?
Sweeping Beauty.

What is the Jekyll and Hyde miracle medicine?
One sip and you're a new man.

What kind of star wears sunglasses?
A movie star.

What did Ebenezer Scrooge say when he bought a sweater?
"Bah, bah, humbug, have you any wool?"

What did E.T. eat at the playground?
Recess Pieces.

What kind of cars do movies stars want to drive?
Os-cars.

What happens when a television writer takes too many baths?
He begins to write soap operas.

Why is it hot after a World Series game?
All the fans have gone.

What turkey was a famous movie star?
Clark Gobble.

What duck was a famous detective?
Duck Tracy.

What's the perfect vision for a space alien?
20/20/20.

Why do vampires drink blood?
Because Coke makes them burp.

Where do football teams buy their new shirts?
In New Jersey.

What movie did Jaws see five times?
"Raiders of the Lost Shark."

What do you call an actor in a suit of armor?
A canned ham.

What happened when the television model put too much mousse on her hair?
She grew antlers.

What is the Eskimo's theme song?
"There's No Business Like Snow Business."

What mouse works for Lipton?
My tea mouse.

What language does Porky the Pig speak?
Pig Latin.

What's Bart Simpson's favorite baseball play?
A Homer.

Why did the elephants laugh at Tarzan?
They thought his nose was funny.

How did Kevin in "Home Alone" know the robbers weren't cat burglars?
His cat wasn't missing.

What kind of entertainment do vampires like?
Something in a jugular vein.

How did Porky the Pig get to the hospital?
In a ham-bulance.

What did E.T.'s mother say to him when he got home?
"Where on earth have you been?"

Why did the TV weather man lose his job?
Because the weather didn't agree with him.

What's the difference between a motion picture and a ski resort?
One has a cast of hundreds and the other has hundreds of casts.

Why didn't the hot dogs want to star in the movies?
Because the rolls weren't good enough.

How does Columbo eat dinner at home?
With a Falk.